Eleanora Jadwin

JACK PRELUTSKY

The Pack Rat's Day

AND OTHER POEMS

ILLUSTRATED BY

Margaret Bloy Graham

MACMILLAN PUBLISHING CO., INC.
New York
COLLIER MACMILLAN PUBLISHERS
London

Macmillan Publishing Co., Inc., 866 Third Avenue, New York, N.Y. 10022
Collier-Macmillan Canada Ltd.
Printed in the United States of America

1   2   3   4   5   6   7   8   9   10

The illustrations are three-color wash drawings. The typeface is
Antique #1 with display set in Bernard Roman.

Library of Congress Cataloging in Publication Data
Prelutsky, Jack   The pack rat's day and other poems.
1. Animals—Juvenile poetry. [1. Animals—Poetry. 2. Humorous poetry]
I. Graham, Margaret Bloy, illus.   II. Title.
PZ8.3.P9Pac   72–81061   ISBN 0–02–775050–7

For
VIC and YETI

THE PACK RAT

The pack rat's day is spent at play

collecting useless stuff.

No matter what the pack rat's got,

he's never got enough.

Nails and tacks and wires and wax,

a knife, a fork, a feather,

large or tiny, dull or shiny,

tin or bone or leather.

Sticks and socks and spoons and rocks

and nuts that squirrels lose,

rings and strings, peculiar things

a rat could never use.

The pack rat saves and stores in caves

strange treasures smooth and knobby.

It's not from greed nor out of need,

he does it as his hobby.

THE BLACK BEAR

In the summer, fall and spring

the black bear sports and has his fling,

but winter sends him straight indoors

and there he snores...and snores...and snores.

THE PLATYPUS

The platypus thought, but his thinking was stuck
when he tried to decide what to be.
He admired the beaver, the mole and the duck
so he borrowed a bit from all three.

The platypus seems to us silly and strange
in his mixed-up and muddled design,
but the platypus wouldn't consider a change
for his singular suit suits him fine.

THE COW

The cow mainly moos as she chooses to moo
and she chooses to moo as she chooses.

She furthermore chews as she chooses to chew
and she chooses to chew as she muses.

If she chooses to moo she may moo to amuse
or may moo just to moo as she chooses.

If she chooses to chew she may moo as she chews
or may chew just to chew as she muses.

THE MOLE

The mole's a solitary soul
who minds his own affairs.
He lives contented in a hole
and rarely goes upstairs.

He's blind, so never sees the earth
but trusts his sense of smell,
and burrowing for all he's worth
the mole does very well.

Although it's dank and dark and small
within the mole's domain
and he must tunnel at a crawl,
the mole does not complain.

While other creatures in his place
might feel the urge to roam,
down in his subterranean base
the mole is right at home.

ELECTRIC EELS

Electric eels are rather rude,

they have a shocking attitude

and generate galvanic jolts

of ergs and amperes, watts and volts.

They don't distinguish friend from foe,

to shock and shock is all they know.

So only foolish people feel

a highly tense electric eel.

THE TWO-HORNED BLACK RHINOCEROS

The two-horned black rhinoceros

has nothing much to say,

and he tends to be unfriendly and unkind.

He's lumpy and he's grumpy

in a thick-skinned sort of way,

and there's nothing but a grumble on his mind.

THE GALLIVANTING GECKO

The gallivanting gecko's ways
are clever and appealing,
he walks up walls and never falls
and trots across the ceiling.

And when he wishes to amaze
the gecko has a knack,
he sheds his tail and without fail
another tail grows back.

THE LION

The lion has a golden mane
and under it a clever brain.
He lies around and idly roars
and lets the lioness do the chores.

THE SKUNK

Whenever you may meet a skunk
at morning, noon or night,
make sure to mind your manners,
be especially polite.

Tip your hat and say hello,
bow deeply from the waist,
tell him that he's handsome
and is dressed in splendid taste.

Agree with anything he says
and smile at every word.
Remark that his opinions
are the best you've ever heard.

Bend over backward for the skunk,
extend him lots of room.
Don't give him any reason
to resort to his perfume!

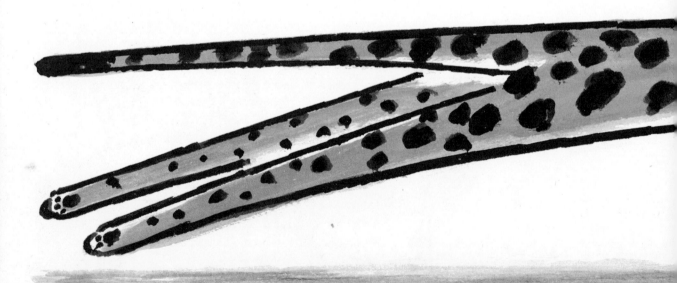

THE CHEETAH

The speedy cheetah loves to run,

he's peerless in a race,

for hardly has the race begun

he's finished in first place.

A blur of fur, he dashes past,

he flashes through the air,

the speedy cheetah runs so fast,

before he's here, he's there.

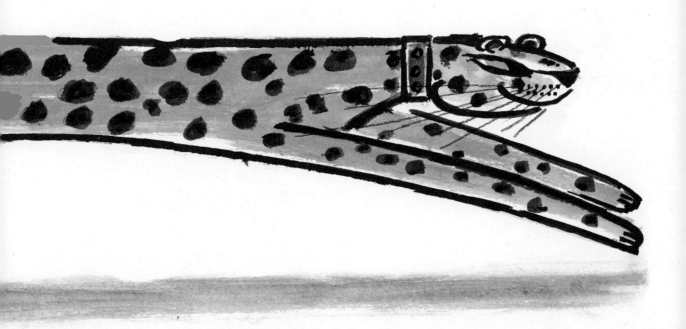

SHEEP

Sheep are gentle, shy and meek.

They love to play at hide-and-seek.

Their hearts are softer than their fleece

and left alone they live in peace.

THE HOUSE MOUSE

Little brown house mouse, laugh and leap,
chitter and cheep while the cat's asleep,
chatter and call and slip through the wall,
trip through the kitchen, skip through the hall.

Little brown house mouse, don't be meek,
dance and squeak and prance and tweak.
There's cheese to take and plenty of cake
so long as you're gone when the cat's awake.

THE CHAMELEON

The changeable chameleon

is forever at his best,

for in any situation

he's appropriately dressed.

Should he stroll through morning flowers

shining golden in the dew,

his attire shortly glitters

with a corresponding hue.

And rambling in the valley

when the meadow grass is green,

he verdantly adjusts himself

and blends into the scene.

In the dim autumnal forest

when the leaves have fallen down,

he corrects his coloration

to a sympathetic brown.

And gazing in the water

he reflects a happy smile,

for the changeable chameleon's

automatically in style.

THE WALRUS

The widdly, waddly walrus
has flippery, floppery feet.
He dives in the ocean for dinner
and stands on his noggin to eat.

The wrinkly, crinkly walrus
swims with a debonair splash.
His elegant tusks are of ivory
and he wears a fine walrus moustache.

The thundery, blundery walrus
has a rubbery, blubbery hide.
He puffs up his neck when it's bedtime
and floats fast asleep on the tide.

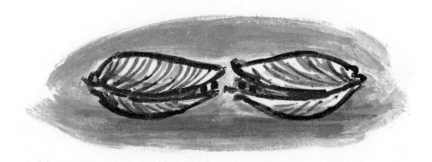

The End